Rosh Hashanah

Julie Murray

Abdo Kids Junior
is an Imprint of Abdo Kids
abdobooks.com

Abdo
HOLIDAYS
Kids

abdobooks.com

Published by Abdo Kids, a division of ABDO, P.O. Box 398166, Minneapolis, Minnesota 55439.
Copyright © 2019 by Abdo Consulting Group, Inc. International copyrights reserved in all countries.
No part of this book may be reproduced in any form without written permission from the publisher.
Abdo Kids Junior™ is a trademark and logo of Abdo Kids.

Printed in the United States of America, North Mankato, Minnesota.

102018

012019

THIS BOOK CONTAINS
RECYCLED MATERIALS

Photo Credits: Getty Images, iStock, Shutterstock, ©Abir Sultan p.7 /EPA-EFE /Shutterstock

Production Contributors: Teddy Borth, Jennie Forsberg, Grace Hansen

Design Contributors: Christina Doffing, Candice Keimig, Dorothy Toth

Library of Congress Control Number: 2018945728

Publisher's Cataloging-in-Publication Data

Names: Murray, Julie, author.

Title: Rosh Hashanah / by Julie Murray.

Description: Minneapolis, Minnesota : Abdo Kids, 2019 | Series: Holidays set 2 |
      Includes glossary, index and online resources (page 24).

Identifiers: ISBN 9781532181740 (lib. bdg.) | ISBN 9781532182723 (ebook) |
      ISBN 9781532183218 (Read-to-me ebook)

Subjects: LCSH: Rosh ha-Shanah--Juvenile literature. | Holidays, festivals, &
      celebrations--Juvenile literature. | Judaism--Juvenile literature. | Jewish New
      Year--Juvenile literature.

Classification: DDC 296.431--dc23

Table of Contents

Rosh Hashanah

Rosh Hashanah is the Jewish New Year. It is a happy time!

It can be in September or October. It lasts for two days.

It is a time to **reflect**. Michael asks for forgiveness.

9

Ben goes to a **synagogue**.

He prays.

A horn is blown. It is loud!

Ruth reads the Torah.

It is holy text.

Mom makes challah bread.

It is yummy!

Levi eats apples. He dips them in honey.

Adam is happy. He is ready for the new year!

Signs of Rosh Hashanah

apples and honey

challah bread

shofar horn

Torah

Glossary

reflect
to think about.

synagogue
a place used by Jews for worship and religious instruction.

Torah
the first part of the Jewish bible, which are the five books of Moses.

Index

Abdo Kids
ONLINE
FREE! ONLINE MULTIMEDIA RESOURCES

Visit abdokids.com and use this code to access crafts, games, videos, and more!

Abdo Kids Code:
HRK1740